GEORGIA
O'KEEFFE

GEORGIA O'KEEFFE

An Adventurous Spirit

BY PHILIP BROOKS

A FIRST BOOK

FRANKLIN WATTS
NEW YORK / CHICAGO / LONDON / TORONTO / SYDNEY

Frontispiece: Georgia O'Keefe in 1929 near "The Pink House" in Taos, New Mexico

Cover art copyright © Collection of The Newark Museum, bequest of
Miss Cora Louise Hartshorn 1958

Photographs copyright ©: NAA–Thomas C. Woods Memorial Collection, Sheldon Memorial
Art Gallery, University of Nebraska–Lincoln, 1958.N-107: p. 10; State Historical Society of
Wisconsin: pp. 12 (WHi-N48-30166), 15 (WHi-X313-2935), 16 (WHi-S65-48); Chatham
Hall, Chatham, Va.: pp. 18, 19; The Art Institute of Chicago: pp. 20, 50 (Alfred Stieglitz
Collection, gift of Georgia O'Keeffe, 1969.835); The Brooklyn Museum: pp. 23 (bequest of
Mary Childs Draper, 77.11), 41 (bequest of Dick S. Ramsay Fund, 58.75), 51 (Estate of Edith
A. Lowenthal, 1992.11.28); The Art Students League: pp. 25, 29 (both Jacob Burckhardt), 26;
The Amon Carter Museum, Ft. Worth, Tex., 5019.4: p. 30; The University of New Mexico Art
Museum, purchase through The Julius L. Rolshoven Memorial Fund with assistance of Friends
of Art, 72.157: p. 31; The Menil Collection, photo by Paul Hester, 85-37 DJ: p. 36;
Panhandle-Plains Historical Society: p. 40; The New Britain Museum of American Art, Conn.:
p. 43; Collection of The Newark Museum, purchase, 1946, J. O'Neill Bequest Fund, 46.157:
p. 45; The Phillips Collection, Washington, D. C.: p. 46; Mitchell Kennerley Papers, Rare
Books and Manuscripts Division, New York Public Library: p. 47; The Carnegie Museum of
Art, Pittsburgh, museum purchase, in memory of Elisabeth Mellon Sellers from her friends,
74.17: p. 49; The Bettmann Archive: p. 53; National Museum of American Art, Smithsonian
Institution, gift of S. C. Johnson and Son, Inc.: p. 57; Indianapolis Museum of Art, Gift of Mr.
and Mrs. James W. Fesler: p. 58.

Library of Congress Cataloging-in-Publication Data

Brooks, Philip, 1963–
Georgia O'Keeffe: an adventurous spirit / by Philip Brooks.
p. cm. — (A First book)
Includes bibliographical references and index.
ISBN 0–531–20182–1
1. O'Keeffe, Georgia, 1887–1986 — Juvenile literature. 2. Artists — United States —
Biography —Juvenile literature. [1. O'Keeffe, Georgia, 1887–1986. 2. Artists.]
I. Title II. Series.

N6537.039B76 1995   94–39333
759. 13 — dc20   CIP AC
[B]

CONTENTS

GEORGIA O'KEEFFE: AN ADVENTUROUS SPIRIT

Georgia O'Keeffe grew up in Sun Prairie, Wisconsin. Her family's farm was surrounded for miles and miles by other farms. In spring, after plowing time, rounded brown hills crisscrossed with deep furrows rolled on as far as she could see. In summer, beautiful fields of grain, and in winter an endless, snow-blanketed expanse, stretched out before her. She could always see the shape of the land. There were no forests to hide the earth, nor oceans to distract from the vastness of the sky.

One winter night, when Georgia was just nine or ten, she spent hours working on the problem of how to draw the snow-covered farm outside her window. The paper was white and so was the farm! Finally, she drew a picture of her window and left all the space inside it white. To her, this was a kind of

Georgia O'Keeffe, with her painting **Horse's Skull with White Rose,** *at an exhibition of her work in 1931.*

magic. She would spend her life working on how best to draw and paint the things she saw and what she felt.

It may seem an odd job to be an artist. When Georgia was a girl, in the late 1800s, it was especially strange for a woman to dream of becoming one. There were certain goals and careers women were not expected to pursue. Women were rarely bankers or blacksmiths. Few women went to medical school and became doctors, or studied law and became lawyers. Women did not run for election to the United States Congress. These jobs were thought to belong to men. Most people never thought about changing that.

As a young woman, in the early 1900s, Georgia attended some of America's finest art schools and studied with some of the greatest teachers. She took anatomy drawing classes where the students learned to draw and paint the human body by studying nude models. Just fifty years earlier, women had not been allowed to do any of these things. Had Georgia been born then, she would have been kept out of these classes and not even been welcomed at social gatherings where male artists smoked cigars, drank whiskey, and discussed important and new ideas in art.

Georgia helped change her world. She did not lead protests against art museums, picketing with signs demanding: "Let Women Paint!" Instead, she worked to create pictures that would earn a place in museums alongside great paintings by men.

In many ways, Georgia O'Keeffe was a stubborn and difficult person. She lived first and foremost for her work. Everything else came after that. Only Georgia's

New York, Night, 1928/29, oil on canvas, 40⅛ x 19⅛ in., by Georgia O'Keeffe

unconquerable will to "say what she meant to say" enabled her to succeed. Her powerful work should be looked at by anyone serious about becoming a painter. Her life, lived with a firm focus on achieving greatness, stands as a work of art in and of itself.

one

NOTICING THE WORLD

On November 15, 1887, in a comfortable white farmhouse near Sun Prairie, Georgia Totto O'Keeffe was born. Her mother's father, George Totto, had come to the United States from Hungary, married a young woman from New York, and settled in Wisconsin. Her father's parents had emigrated from Ireland and made their way to Sun Prairie, where they began farming—for a time as neighbors of the Totto family. In 1884, Ida Totto and Frank O'Keeffe were married.

Georgia was the second oldest of the seven children born to the O'Keeffes. Her description of an early memory shows that even at a very young age, she had an artist's eye. She noticed colors and patterns and, especially, light. In her recollection, she told of being carried outside when about a year old and being placed on a bright patterned quilt. It was

The O'Keeffe family home near Sun Prairie, Wisconsin

"an afternoon in the late fall in the brightness of outdoor life. . . . I was looking all around, at the brightness of the light. I remember the light, our unusually big pillows, the quilt I was on and the ground beyond. It all seemed so new and I started going toward it. I clearly remember my mother snatching me up and sticking me down in the pillows so I couldn't get out. I remember my annoyance at not being able to get to the brightness of the light beyond, and my struggle to get there. . . ." This struggle to "get to the light" is one she pursued her entire life as she labored to make colored paint appear as light captured on a canvas.

Georgia always noticed the way light and shadows played upon the objects around her. Her first day of school left her with memories, not of the other children or the teacher, nor of the butterflies in her stomach, but of the walk there. It was a muddy spring morning and she stopped to look at the deep ruts passing wagons had left in the rich brown mud of the road, the way the ruts filled with water that sparkled in the sun. The colors and patterns of nature made her stop and look. Sometimes she spent hours staring at a single flower until she became lost in its little world.

Georgia recalled her childhood as a happy one. Although her father sometimes drank too much, she loved spending time with him. On walks in the family fields, he taught her to notice how changes in the season changed the way the land and sky looked. In fall, the sky took on a darker blue, and the grass became like green velvet. The land and sky changed every moment if she watched carefully.

Georgia enjoyed listening to her father sing and play his fiddle. He taught Georgia to love music. Her mother, too, was musical, and played the piano and sang. Later Georgia would describe some of her abstract paintings as "music made into a picture."

She also liked to spend time by herself, playing with a simple dollhouse she had made. Just as when she gazed at a flower, she could lose herself for hours in the miniature dollhouse world.

At bedtime, her mother read adventure tales aloud, stories about cowboys and Indians in the vast deserts of the Wild West. Georgia went to sleep each night imagining this strange place where tumbleweeds blew across the land and the blue sky went on forever. It was the idea of a new land where almost no people lived for miles and miles that intrigued her. She liked the idea of being on her own, needing no one.

When she was nearly five, Georgia started school in the same one-room schoolhouse where her parents had gone as children. But Ida O'Keeffe wanted a more complete education for Georgia and her sisters than she had gotten. Ida wanted her daughters to become cultured young women who knew about beauty. She arranged for the three oldest girls to take private art lessons. Every Saturday, Georgia, Anita, and Ida, the three oldest O'Keeffe girls climbed into a horse and buggy and rode seven bumpy, clattering miles into town. In those days, to travel seven miles was something of an expedition. The roads were rutted clay and mud.

In town, the art teacher taught her students to use watercolors to copy pictures she kept in a cup-

In the 1890s, many children in rural Wisconsin attended one-room schoolhouses similar to this one, whose students and teacher lined up to pose for the photographer.

board. Georgia found she enjoyed painting with watercolors even more than drawing. But it was when she got home and made up pictures of her own to paint that she became inspired. She was tired of copying things other people made up. She could spend hours and hours drawing and hardly notice that it was getting dark outside, or that her father had come in from the fields, or that her sisters were playing a game without her.

*The trip to town, by horse and buggy
over country roads*

She made pictures of the Wild West, of tropical islands in the South Seas, of a lighthouse—places and things she'd never seen. It seemed magical to be able to conjure images onto paper, to take a simple pencil or paints and be able to make things which, it seemed to her, were somehow alive. It was as if she were drawing or painting everything she felt at that moment.

From her first efforts, Georgia had very particular ideas about how her pictures should look. She became angry when the teacher looked at one of her paintings and "fixed" something.

two

"QUEEN" OF THE STUDIO

When Georgia was fifteen, the O'Keeffes sold the farm in Wisconsin and moved to Williamsburg, Virginia. Once there, Ida enrolled Georgia in a girls' boarding school. At Chatham Hall Episcopal Institute, high school girls studied everything they were thought to need to become elegant ladies and get married. The other girls were at first a little put off by Georgia. They wore fitted dresses decorated with big bows and ruffles, while Georgia, the Wisconsin farm girl, sewed her own very plain dresses. Her hair was pulled back in a tight braid. Her accent set her apart even more. The students thought she was stuck up and odd, but when they got to know her, they found she was funny, smart, and mischievous. She enjoyed practical jokes and drew caricatures of their teachers. They also respected her and understood she was seri-

A scene from Georgia's days at Chatham Hall Episcopal Institute: The school principal catches Georgia (second from right) and three classmates in the midst of some mischief.

ous about her art. They believed that if any woman could become a famous artist, it would be Georgia.

Georgia loved Chatham's art studio. It had big windows and plenty of space. She painted at an easel set in the middle of the room. Some of the other girls were jealous. They thought Georgia acted like the "queen" of the studio. She stared for minutes at a time preparing to make a single brushstroke, unaware of the chattering and movement around her.

Chatham had many rules for student behavior, which led Georgia to look for ways to bend or break them. She took friends on long walks into the nearby woods and encouraged them to take off their shoes and dangle their feet in a cold stream. She was amazed they had never thought to try it! The school might have worried she was a troublemaker, but her art teacher saw her as a true talent. She approved of the choice when the other girls made Georgia editor of the school yearbook.

Georgia drew this illustration for the 1905 Chatham yearbook, **The Mortar-Board.**

*Two early photographs from the Art Institute of
Chicago show the building as it looked at about
the time Georgia studied there, and also a
life-drawing class of the period.*

Near the end of her two years at Chatham, a friend came into the art studio and found Georgia burning many of her watercolors and drawings. Her friend was horrified. All that work—ruined! Georgia explained that when she became famous she did not want anyone to see her early failures. It would be too embarrassing.

At seventeen, Georgia went on to take classes at the prestigious Art Institute of Chicago. Georgia's mother was considered very liberal to allow her daughter to attend an art school where women could draw from nude models. At one of her early classes at the Art Institute, a young man posed wearing only a loincloth. Georgia became terribly embarrassed, and blushing, left the room. Many years later, Georgia claimed that all she learned at the Art Institute was to be able to stay in the same room with a nude model. She was never interested in painting the human figure. Unlike many other artists, she painted few portraits, even of the people she loved.

three

NEW YORK CITY

*I*n 1906, while visiting her family in Virginia, Georgia became very ill with typhoid fever. It left her thin and weak, and her sisters had to nurse her back to health. When she was ready to return to art school, she chose to go to New York City, instead of Chicago. She believed the most important art in the United States was being made there and she wanted to see and learn about the best ideas of the time.

New York in the early 1900s was an exciting place. Taller and taller buildings were being constructed. The longest bridge in the world, a miracle of engineering, had recently opened, linking the island of Manhattan with what was the city of Brooklyn. Poets, writers, painters, and musicians flocked to New York City and began to create art that reflected the excitement and rapid changes going on

In 1948 Georgia would paint The Brooklyn Bridge, *oil on masonite, 47¹⁵⁄₁₆ x 35⅞ in., creating her own image of the graceful structure.*

around them, rather than imitating work being done across the Atlantic, in Paris and London.

Artists in America had always looked to Europe for ideas. The United States was still a young country and did not yet have its own tradition of great art. But its youth and lack of tradition made it a place brimming with energy and the freedom to try new things. Artists stayed up nights talking about how to get onto paper or canvas, or into music or sculpture, a feeling of what it was like to live in America, to be surrounded by new ideas and technological changes hardly imagined just a decade earlier. Art based on work done by Europeans expressed ideas and feelings of an "old world." In New York City, artists felt on the verge of creating something "American."

Georgia was excited by all this, maybe a little overwhelmed. She was only nineteen years old. She enrolled at the Art Students League and studied with a number of teachers, including William Merritt Chase. Chase was a forceful teacher and a colorful person. He encouraged his students to work quickly and with color, energy, and individuality. Georgia found some of his ideas about painting confining, yet she learned a lot from him. He taught her to use more white to make her pictures bright. She also learned how to paint still-lifes—pictures of fruit and

At New York's Art Students League, Georgia studied still-life painting with William Merritt Chase, seen here conducting a class about 1907.

vegetables, flower arrangements, or copper pots and pans. She learned how to create the illusion of three dimensions on a flat canvas. Later she would paint more abstract pictures—pictures that did not try to show a person's face, or a landscape, or a bowl of fruit, but were concerned more with shapes and col-

Georgia's student painting, **Dead Rabbit and Copper Pot,** *1908, oil on canvas, 19 x 23½ in., won the approval of Chase, her teacher, and she was awarded a scholarship for the League's summer school at Lake George, New York.*

ors. However, the experience of learning a disciplined and formal approach helped Georgia become a better artist. Just as a basketball player lifts weights to get stronger, and runs to gain endurance, as well as practicing a jump shot, an artist does exercises to build a foundation of skills to use in later work.

four

TWO GREAT TEACHERS

One afternoon, some of the art students went to see an exhibit at a gallery called "291" (from the address of a brownstone building on Fifth Avenue where the gallery originated). The gallery was run by a famous photographer and art critic, Alfred Stieglitz (STEE-glits). At 291 the students saw drawings by Auguste Rodin, a French artist. The drawings appeared to Georgia to be nothing more than a few curved lines and random scratches. Some viewers even charged that Rodin had drawn them with his eyes closed! Several of Georgia's classmates began a debate with Stieglitz over the merits of Rodin's drawings. They had more old-fashioned ideas about what made a great drawing.

Stieglitz listened to the students, staring into their eyes from behind his small glasses perched atop his nose. Then he turned red with anger as he tore their arguments to shreds. He insisted these drawings were of "a human soul," something about which they knew nothing at all. The outburst made Georgia uncomfortable, but she admired Stieglitz for his strong feelings for the art and the artists he believed in.

During these years, the O'Keeffe family situation was becoming very difficult. Georgia's father had used the money from the sale of the Sun Prairie farm to start a business manufacturing hollow concrete blocks for construction. But no one wanted the blocks. The O'Keeffes had to sell the home they had bought in Williamsburg. And, adding to their sadness, Georgia's mother was ill with tuberculosis.

Georgia's brothers and her father, now drinking more heavily, built a new home out of the concrete blocks. The place was ugly and uncomfortable. To help with their living expenses, her parents began renting rooms to boarders. Since there was no money for her to return to the Art Students League, Georgia had to put aside her plans. She went to live with an aunt in Chicago and took a job as a commercial illustrator, drawing pictures of lace and dresses, twelve hours a day, six days a week.

The period Georgia spent working in Chicago was surely a hard time for her and, to make the situation worse, she got sick again. This time it was a very

Eugene Speicher, a classmate at the League,
painted Portrait of Georgia O'Keeffe *in 1908,*
oil on canvas, 21½ x 17½ in.

bad case of measles and her eyesight was affected. Georgia went back to Virginia—to Charlottesville, where her family had moved to find a healthier climate for her mother. When Georgia recovered, her sisters persuaded her to enroll in a summer art class (open to women) at the nearby University of Virginia.

Her teacher in Virginia was Alon Bement. Bement's approach to making paintings was influenced by ideas from China and Japan. These cultures produced art that emphasized composition and strength from simplicity. These Asian cultures also embraced the idea of "life as art." This idea was an important one for Georgia. She believed it was "of use to everyone— whether you think of it consciously or not. . . . Where you have the windows and doors in a house. How you address a letter and put on the stamp. What shoes you choose and how you comb your hair." Throughout her life, Georgia made her home a work of art. She did not clutter her rooms, using a few carefully chosen objects

The simplicity and sense of order Georgia valued can be seen in her work and in the places where she lived—such as here, in her cherished home in Abiquiu, New Mexico.

Tent Door at Night, *1913, watercolor*

to create an environment where she could think and work. The clothes she wore were simple and elegant. She carried herself with quiet dignity.

Alon Bement's specialty was composition, the way a picture occupies the square or rectangular space of its canvas. He believed one should compose pictures by dividing a canvas into large geometric shapes—circles and triangles. One of Georgia's most famous early paintings, *Tent Door at Night,* follows this idea. Without its title, we might never guess what it was. Its beauty is in the color and strong triangles created by the tent.

At the end of the summer, Georgia accepted an offer to teach art in the public schools of Amarillo, Texas. Here she found the Wild-West landscapes of her mother's stories. The vast prairies and deserts, the tumbleweeds and sagebrush, captured her imagination once again. She loved the way Texas looked and found she enjoyed teaching, but to become a real artist, she felt she had to return to New York City.

In the fall of 1914, once again in New York, Georgia enrolled at Columbia Teachers College. She took art classes with Arthur Wesley Dow, whose book, *Composition*, had given Alon Bement many of his ideas. Another student in Dow's classes was Anita Pollitzer. She and Georgia had met while at the New York Art Students League. Their friendship was solidified by the excitement they shared in response to Dow's ideas.

After paying for rent and Dow's classes, Georgia had little money. Pollitzer wrote years later that "even though Georgia had no money, her brushes were always the best and her colors the brightest." She was willing to eat less to have good paints.

Both Pollitzer and O'Keeffe visited Alfred Stieglitz's gallery regularly to see the latest work he was showing. Georgia had come to respect Stieglitz as someone of vision, someone who knew which new art had true value before history decided it was good. Much of the work Stieglitz admired looked unusual, even ugly, at the time but later became famous and valued by the world. This is often true. It takes bravery both to make something really new and different, and also to look at new work with an open mind. Artists risk having people say their work is poor, or even that they are crazy! These brave artists need someone like Stieglitz—a person with a reputation for intelligence and good taste, to stand up and explain that the new paintings (or sculptures, or poems) are truly good if only one learns to look at them with "new eyes."

five

"A WOMAN ON PAPER"

In 1915, needing money, Georgia accepted an offer to teach art at a college in Columbia, South Carolina. She hated to leave New York and thought Columbia was the most boring place in the world. In some ways, however, Columbia turned out to be good for her. She spent a lot of time alone thinking about her own work as compared to the work of the artists she'd seen at 291. She hung up all her pictures in her studio and looked at them. She was not happy with a single one. She wrote to Anita Pollitzer: "[I have] things in my head that are not like what anyone has taught me—shapes and ideas so near to me—so natural to my way of being and thinking that it hasn't occurred to me to put them down."

She set aside her old paintings and drawings and started again. In October 1915, she wrote to

Anita: "I am starting all over new—Have put everything I have ever done away and don't expect to get any of it out ever again—or for a long time anyway. I feel disgusted with it all and glad I'm disgusted."

All the years and hours of hard work had brought her, she now believed, to the real beginning of her work. She packed up her bright oil paints, watercolors, and brushes, and began again, with paper and charcoal.

In black and white, she began creating new and strange shapes and images. She drew and drew, day and night. She tacked the work to the walls and covered the floor with these pictures which seemed to come from the deepest part of her mind and body.

When she stepped back and looked at what she'd done, she was happy and excited. The pictures seemed original and true to her own natural way of seeing and feeling. She wanted to show them to somebody so she rolled up a few, put them in a cardboard tube, and mailed them to Anita Pollitzer in New York. The only instructions she gave were that Anita show the pictures to no one else.

Anita wrote back to Georgia: "Astounded and awfully happy were my feelings today when I opened the batch of drawings. I tell you I felt them! & when I say that I mean that. . . ."

Charcoal No. 9, 1915, charcoal on paper, 25 x 19⅛ in., one of Georgia's strong and dramatic charcoal drawings

Anita was too excited to pay attention to Georgia's instructions. She showed the drawings to Alfred Stieglitz. Stieglitz stood and studied each one. "At last!" he said. "A woman on paper." He believed she had found a way of drawing that was somehow feminine—not in a girlish or sentimental way, but in a manner that spoke of strength and sensitivity.

"What woman did these?" he asked at last.

"Georgia O'Keeffe, my friend," Anita said.

"Will you tell her for me," he said quietly, "that this is the purest, most sincere work to enter Gallery 291 in a long while."

Georgia was angry that Anita had shown the work to Stieglitz but was pleased by his response. She kept working long hours. She wrote Anita: "I've been working like mad all day—had a great time—Anita it seems I never had such a good time—I was just trying to say what I wanted to say—and it is so much fun to say what you want to—I worked till my head all felt tight in the top—then I stopped and looked, Anita—and do you know—I really doubted the soundness of the mentality of a person who can work so hard and laugh like I did and get such genuine fun out of that sort of thing—who can make anything like that [a drawing] as seriously as I did. Anita—do you suppose I'm crazy?"

Throughout her life Georgia would create in the same way. For a period she produced great numbers of works—then, for weeks or even months, frustrated and tired, she produced nothing.

In the spring of 1916, Georgia returned to New York to complete her degree at Columbia University. While eating lunch in the university's cafeteria she heard that an exhibit at Gallery 291 featured the drawings of "Virginia O'Keeffe." Georgia was sure the drawings were hers, that Stieglitz had hung them without her permission. In a rage, she hurried to the gallery and found she was right. She demanded to speak to Alfred Stieglitz, but he was away on jury duty. She returned the next day and demanded that Stieglitz explain himself. He had no right, she said, to show her pictures without her permission. He admitted it was wrong but argued they were so beautiful he had been unable to stop himself. There was a loud argument between them, but in the end, Georgia allowed the pictures to remain on exhibit.

Georgia then began to wonder why Stieglitz and Pollitzer were so impressed by her simple charcoal drawings. Throughout her life, even after she had become famous, she wondered why people liked her work and whether they liked it for reasons that were somehow "wrong." This kind of self-doubt plagues many artists and perhaps spurs them on to create even greater work.

six

GEORGIA AND ALFRED

Impressed by Georgia's honesty, intelligence, strength of character, and beauty, but most of all by her work, Stieglitz fell in love with her. As the years passed, their long romance became nearly as famous as their work. Stieglitz's many photographs of O'Keeffe are among the most beautiful and powerful he ever took.

In the fall of 1916, Georgia left New York to take a teaching job at a college in western Texas. She and Stieglitz kept in touch, trading photographs, paintings, and letters. Georgia found the Texas desert absolutely inspiring. She wrote to Stieglitz of "the terrible winds and . . . wonderful emptiness."

She began to perfect her technical methods in Texas. She started using a glass palette, which could be cleaned easily and thoroughly, so her colors remained pure. For the same reason she used a dif-

At West Texas State Normal College, Georgia filled the art room with teaching aids she had sent from New York: Japanese prints, pottery, and photographs of textiles and designs.

ferent brush for each color. She kept careful records on index cards of every color she mixed so she could use it again in later paintings. She applied paint with the tiniest possible brushstrokes. She wanted them to be invisible.

Georgia was also becoming more sure of her subject matter—exactly what it was she wanted to paint. It seemed natural to her now to make pictures of sunsets, barns, and the desert. She was imitating no one—not even herself. She experimented with scale, making huge pictures of small flowers, and small pictures of vast desert landscapes.

She took long walks to watch the slow and brilliant Texas sunsets. She painted watercolors of what she saw on her walks. Watercolor was the perfect medium for these pictures, as it dries very quickly. This forces the painter to work fast and create more of a sketch, an impression, rather than a careful

Blue No. 3, 1916, watercolor on tissue paper, 15⅞ x 10¹⁵⁄₁₆ in.

painting. Georgia began with what she saw, then painted how seeing it made her feel. This filtering of the outside world through her feelings brought Georgia much closer than her earlier work to how she wanted to paint. It felt "true."

In 1918, Stieglitz asked Georgia to move back to New York so they could be together. She agreed. Six years later, after Stieglitz and his first wife were divorced, he and Georgia were married. Georgia did not take Alfred's name. She wished to maintain her own identity and independence. In fact, some of their friends jokingly called Alfred "Mr. O'Keeffe."

Georgia and Alfred lived high up in the Shelton Hotel, one of the new steel-framed skyscrapers of Manhattan. Georgia painted views of the Hudson River as seen from her apartment windows. She also painted the building, seen from the sidewalk, with the bright sun bursting behind it. Georgia saw natural beauty in the middle of the busiest city in the world. Even these city pictures seem to be about the wide spaces and clean light of the desert. The buildings become like hills and mountains. Few people inhabit Georgia's New York landscape.

Georgia believed technology was causing every-thing in the city to move too fast. Unlike painters who celebrate machines and speed, Georgia tried to make people stop and truly look at nature. About a painting

East River from the 30th Story of the Shelton Hotel,
1928, oil on canvas, 30 x 48 in.

of a red flower done during this period she later wrote:
"That was in the '20s and everything was going so fast.
Nobody had time to reflect. . . . Well, the flower was
perfectly exquisite, but it was so small you really could
not appreciate it for itself. So then and there I decided
to paint the flower in a huge scale, then you could not
ignore its beauty. . . ."

She continued painting flowers on a large scale. Today we see her images printed on calendars, postcards, and posters. We are used to seeing the big Jack-in-the-pulpits, cannas, and poppies. When she painted them, however, this distortion of scale was a startling new idea.

Georgia was happy when she and Alfred could leave the city for the summer. They spent the hot months at his family's summer home in Lake George, New York. Georgia was more comfortable in the country but was often overwhelmed by her husband's family and by constant visitors. So many people in the house sometimes made it impossible to find the peace and privacy she needed for her work.

Still, Lake George was far from the distractions of New York City, where Alfred's gallery was always crowded with artists wanting help and advice. Georgia often found herself in the midst of petty arguments and jealousies. Some male painters in Stieglitz's circle, for example, criticized her for using bright colors, or referred to her scornfully as a "woman painter."

During the country summers she put these bothers aside. She picked strawberries and took long walks. She swam. Stieglitz took many photographs of her. He found her an endlessly interesting subject, long and lean, her face full of character.

White Flower on Red Earth No. 1, *1943,*
oil on canvas, 26 x 30¼ in.

At Lake George, she painted big pictures of
tiny wildflowers, and also abstract pictures that
seemed to be about the water and wind, trees and
stones. Other times, she painted the rolling hills and
old barns in sharp clear colors and well-defined
lines. She narrowed her focus more and more to sub-

jects that attracted her—Jack-in-the-pulpits, hills and sky, the water of the lake.

Stieglitz and O'Keeffe influenced one another. They often chose the same subjects—the mountains and sky, a farmhouse, a barn door. The way she composed many of her pictures is repeated in some of Alfred's photographs. Neither one "copied" the other. The two were learning from each other, finding different ways to see things and to show what they'd seen.

My Shanty, Lake George, *1922*, oil on canvas, *20 x 27 in.*

In 1923 Stieglitz photographed Georgia's one-person show, "One Hundred Pictures," at a New York gallery.

When the summers ended, they returned to New York. Walking together, they were a striking couple. Both usually dressed in black in the city. Stieglitz wore a cape, his white hair wild in the wind. Georgia was tall and mysterious-looking, with her hair pulled back in a braid and her high collar buttoned up to her chin.

seven

A SPIRITUAL HOME

Georgia often grew weary of her life in New York and felt the need of emotional and physical independence. Some friends had moved to New Mexico and asked her to come. They described the area as the most beautiful, magical place they'd ever seen. In the summer of 1929, she went for a long visit. She went first to Santa Fe, and then to Taos, a small colony in the high plains, ringed by mountains, that was famous as the place where the writer D. H. Lawrence had lived.

As her train steamed through the desert, she felt that she was headed home. She felt a deep connection to the brown land which stretched seemingly forever under the vast blue sky. She was elated and inspired to begin working.

Her friends lent her a studio. It was a round little structure made of adobe (a-DOE-bee), a mixture

**Gate of Adobe Church, *1929, oil on canvas,*
*20$\frac{1}{16}$ x 16 in.***

of clay, straw, sand, and water. Adobe is a common building material in New Mexico. Georgia liked its tan color and smooth texture. She painted many pictures of adobe houses and churches.

She went horseback riding nearly every day. She loved the huge distances of the desert. She could

Blue and Green Music, 1919, oil on canvas, 23 x 19 in.

ride for miles and look back and still see her friends' ranch and her little studio. She loved to watch the hills turn orange then purple in the sunset.

Georgia, like all painters, struggled to control many different elements when making a painting. Each work requires the correct technique—composition, line, brushstrokes, colors, and so on—to make a pleasing picture. But a true artist understands his or her own thoughts and feelings about the subject, and manages to express them in the work so that others may feel the same things. Georgia was gaining control over the art of painting, and just as importantly, was more and more able to tap her deepest feelings and express them in color, line, and composition.

At the end of the summer, Georgia was reluctant to return to New York. She felt she had found a spiritual home in New Mexico, but she also had strong ties to Stieglitz. She filled a wooden crate with cow bones and skulls she'd found in the desert to take back with her to New York for inspiration.

Ram's Head, White Hollyhock-Hills, *1935,*
oil, 30 x 36 in.

The bones didn't remind her of death. She liked the way they looked—their odd shapes, textures, and pale color. She included the bones in many paintings. She felt she learned from them how different forms and shapes must be painted to look three-dimensional on a flat canvas. They reminded her of the clean white light of the Taos summer.

From this time on, Georgia and Alfred had the same discussion every spring. He wanted her to go with him to Lake George. Georgia always ended up in New Mexico. She loved Alfred and knew he needed her, but she needed her time in the desert. For many artists, their work is so demanding of their time, energy, and thought, that they lose, or set aside, other areas of their lives.

Georgia was just beginning her greatest artistic work. Alfred, however, was growing old. He was twenty-three years older than Georgia. In 1946, at age eighty-two, he had a massive stroke and did not recover. Alfred's death made Georgia very sad. In addition to being her husband, he had been her friend and partner; he had advised and encouraged her, and helped her manage her career.

No one ever replaced Alfred in Georgia's life. A number of lifelong friends and her sisters visited often, but more and more she wanted to be alone. With the help of several friends and admirers, includ-

Stieglitz and O'Keeffe in the 1940s at An American Place, Stieglitz's gallery at that time.

ing a young photographer named Doris Bry, she spent months sorting through Alfred's own photographs and the paintings he'd collected. Bry and Georgia devoted much time and energy to ensuring that the world would be aware of and understand his huge contribution to art.

eight

GHOST RANCH AND ABIQUIU

I n 1949, at the age of sixty-two, Georgia moved to Abiquiu, New Mexico, a remote spot near Ghost Ranch, a place where she had often spent her summers. She had bought and restored an old adobe house and installed a studio in the stable. She devoted the rest of her life to her work, with few interruptions.

Four years later, she made her first trip to Europe. When she had the opportunity to meet the artist Pablo Picasso, she refused, saying they would not be able to speak to one another as she spoke only English and he spoke Spanish and French. She avoided public meetings with other artists, which she regarded a waste of time.

Georgia continued traveling, taking a major trip every other year until she was in her nineties, but at home she was famous for her wish to keep out of

A 1920 photograph of the plaza in Abiquiu, New Mexico, where Georgia lived and worked from 1949 until her death.

the public eye. People who loved her work sometimes came to Abiquiu, hoping for a glimpse of Georgia tending her garden, or taking a walk in her long black dress. She lived quite well but not extravagantly. She had help in her household, bought a good car, and had nice things, but still enjoyed growing much of her own food, living simply, and working. "I prefer to live as bare as possible," she said.

Through her seventies, Georgia's energy never failed her. However, her vision gradually began to fail. Still, at seventy-five, after an airplane trip, she hung several enormous canvases in her garage and painted the largest works of her career. They were pictures of clouds as one might see them from an airplane window. "It is breathtaking," she said, "as one rises up over the world one has been living in . . . and looks down at it stretching away and away. . . ." Today, the pictures hang in the Art Institute of Chicago, where she began her professional training.

Perhaps Georgia loved plane rides because she could see the land without people on it. She found most people—aside from her friends—an annoying bother. There are many stories of her unfriendliness to visitors. Once, a group of art students approached her near the gate to her house. "What is it?" she asked.

"We'd like to see Georgia O'Keeffe," a girl answered.

Georgia faced the group. "Okay," she said, showing them herself. "Here's the front," she said. Then she turned abruptly to go, saying over her shoulder, "And the back!"

She was very demanding to work for. Everything had to be done exactly her way, and so she went through a number of secretaries and house-

Only One, *1959, oil on canvas, 36 x 30⅛ in.*

The Gray Hills, *1942, oil on canvas, 20 x 30 in. Georgia often painted scenes of the desert landscapes near her home.*

keepers. Then one day a young potter named Juan Hamilton, who was working in the kitchen at Ghost Ranch, showed up at her door. Perhaps with his intense gaze and droopy mustache, he reminded her of a young Alfred Stieglitz. For whatever reason, she did not turn him away. After he boxed several of her paintings—as carefully as she herself would have done—she let him begin to help her with her responsibilities. Gradually, they formed a close friendship and Georgia came to depend on him. As Hamilton gained influence in Georgia's life, her friends worried that he was taking advantage of her growing frailty. Still, he appeared to have comforted her in her last years, and was loyal to her and devoted to her work.

Except for trips abroad, Georgia was absolutely attached to New Mexico, her garden, and the Native Americans who lived near her. She continued to paint the desert—churches, barns, bones, mountains, hills, flowers—well into her eighties. Her work sold for large sums of money and she was famous throughout the world.

By the age of ninety-six she was blind. She spent her last days sitting serenely in a chair, feeling the changing light of day on her face. She died peacefully at ninety-eight. Her ashes were scattered to the wind near her house.

Georgia O'Keeffe created a rich and impressive body of work. Just as impressive was her will, her drive to make pictures she loved. She always painted for herself, because she loved to paint, not to be rich and famous—although she surely enjoyed her success. Any number of times, she might have given up before she found her own way to paint what she wanted to say. As a woman, she faced even greater discouragement than male artists would have. She recognized that she had chosen a difficult path, but was never afraid to try and fail. Every person who has ever done anything new and creative has risked looking like a fool. Alfred Stieglitz might have laughed at those first drawings Anita Pollitzer showed him. Georgia O'Keeffe's work might never have been appreciated by anyone.

Georgia's life demonstrates that persistence, patience, and stubborn confidence in one's own vision might lead to a life filled with turmoil, struggle, a kind of loneliness, but also love and the deepest sort of satisfaction—the realization of one's personal dreams.

FOR FURTHER READING

Ball, Jacqueline and Catherine Conant. *Georgia O'Keeffe: Painter of the Desert.* Woodbridge, CT: Blackbirch, 1991.

Berry, Michael. *Georgia O'Keeffe.* New York: Chelsea House, 1988.

Gherman, Beverly. *Georgia O'Keeffe: The Wideness and Wonder of Her World.* New York: Macmillan, 1986.

Sills, Leslie. *Inspirations: Stories about Women Artists: Georgia O'Keeffe, Frida Kahlo, Alice Neel, Faith Ringgold.* Niles, IL: Whitman, 1989.

Turner, Robyn M. *Georgia O'Keeffe: Portraits of Women Artists for Children.* Boston: Little, Brown, 1993.

Georgia O'Keeffe (Videorecording produced by WNET/13) Chicago: Home Vision, 1977.

INDEX

ABOUT THE AUTHOR

Philip Brooks is a writer from Chicago, where he lives with his wife Balinda. He received a master's degree in fiction writing from the University of Iowa, and his stories have appeared in various magazines. He claims that he would rather be a painter, or a pro basketball player, than a writer. Unfortunately, he can neither draw nor jump.